CW00498448

MARGARET RIZZA

JUST CHANTS

kevin mayhew

We hope you enjoy *Just Chants*. Further copies are available from your local Kevin Mayhew stockist.

In case of difficulty, or to request a catalogue, please contact the publisher direct by writing to:

The Sales Department
KEVIN MAYHEW LTD
Buxhall
Stowmarket
Suffolk IP14 3BW

Phone 01449 737978
Fax 01449 737834
E-mail info@kevinmayhewltd.com

First published in Great Britain in 2003 by Kevin Mayhew Ltd.

ISBN 1 84417 068 3
ISMN M 57024 197 2
Catalogue No: 1450282

0 1 2 3 4 5 6 7 8 9

Cover design by Angela Selfe

Music proof reader: Linda Ottewell

Printed and bound in Great Britain

Important Copyright Information

The Publishers wish to express their gratitude to the copyright owners who have granted permission to include their copyright material in this book. Full details are indicated on the respective pages.

The **words** of most of the songs in this publication are covered by a **Church Copyright Licence** which is available from Christian Copyright Licensing International. This allows local church reproduction on overhead projector acetates, in service bulletins, songsheets, audio/visual recording and other formats.

The **music** in this book is covered by the additional **Music Reproduction Licence** which is issued by CCLI in the territories of Europe and Australasia. You may photocopy the music and words of the songs in the book provided:

You hold a current Music Reproduction Licence from CCLI.

The copyright owner of the song you intend to photocopy is included in the Authorised Catalogue List which comes with your Music Reproduction Licence.

The Music Reproduction Licence is **not** currently available in the USA or Canada.

Full details of CCLI can be obtained from their Web site (www.ccli.com) or you can contact them direct at the following offices:

Christian Copyright Licensing (Europe) Ltd
PO Box 1339, Eastbourne, East Sussex, BN21 1AD, UK
Tel: +44 (0)1323 417711; Fax: +44 (0)1323 417722; E-mail: info@ccli.co.uk

CCL Asia-Pacific Pty Ltd (Australia and New Zealand)
PO Box 6644, Baulkham Hills Business Centre, NSW 2153, Australia
Tel: +61 (02) 9894-5386; Toll Free Phone: 1-800-635-474
Fax: +61 (02) 9894-5701; Toll Free Fax: 1-800-244-477
E-mail executive@ccli.co.au

Christian Copyright Licensing Inc
17201 NE Sacramento Street, Portland, Oregon 97230, USA
Tel: +1 (503) 257 2230; Toll Free Phone: 1 (800) 234 2446;
Fax: +1 (503) 257 2244; E-mail executive@ccli.com

Foreword

Just Chants is drawn from the four collections, *Fountain of Life, Fire of Love, River of Peace* and *Light in Our Darkness.* The chants are all in voice-friendly keys and have SATB choral parts.

There are many ways to explore when you come to sing these chants. Humming can be used at the beginning or end of the chants and can also be used to accompany a solo voice or an instrumental variation. Unison female voices can be used alternating with male voices. The choral parts can be interspersed with solo, unison chanting or instrumental variations.

All the instrumental variations can be found in the full scores and in one or two cases where the keys have been put down to allow for extra vocal ease, the instrumental variations can be found in the relative keys in *Chants and Songs*, a collection of simplified unison arrangements, each one having a C instrument and a B♭ instrument variation.

Ideally, the chants should be memorised, enabling them to make the longest journey in the world – from head to heart. In this way the repetitive nature of the chant becomes a preparation for prayer, enabling the mind to be still and calm while the heart is allowed to open itself to the indwelling Spirit, the risen Christ, deep within our being – the gateway to love and peace.

> So come to him, our living stone, the stone rejected by men but chosen by God and precious to him; set yourselves close to him and let yourselves be built, as living stones, into a spiritual temple.
>
> You are a chosen race, a royal priesthood, a consecrated nation, a people set apart to sing the praises of God who called you out of darkness into his wonderful light.
>
> (1 Peter 2:4-6)

MARGARET RIZZA

Contents

IN GOD ALONE

Text: Psalm 61(62)
Music: Margaret Rizza

(♩ = 72)
Dm Gm C7 F B♭ B♭/E Gm
S
A
In God a-lone is my soul at rest; he a-lone is my
T
B
A7 Dm D7 Gm Csus4 C7 F
rock, my strength; in God a-lone is my soul at rest;
Last time
B♭maj7 Em7(♭5) Dm/F Gm/A A Dm/F Gm Asus4 A Dm
he a-lone is my rock, he is my strength. He a-lone, he is my strength.

VENI, SANCTE SPIRITUS

Come, Holy Spirit

Text: Traditional

Music: Margaret Rizza

CHANT TRIO: add a part on each repetition

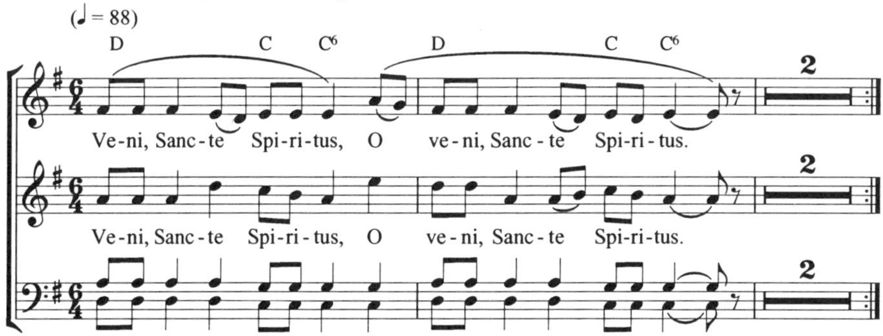
(♩ = 88)
D C C6 D C C6
2
Ve-ni, Sanc-te Spi-ri-tus, O ve-ni, Sanc-te Spi-ri-tus.
2
Ve-ni, Sanc-te Spi-ri-tus, O ve-ni, Sanc-te Spi-ri-tus.
2

VOCAL ACCOMPANIMENT

D C Cmaj7 D C D/A C6 D/A C6
S
A
Sanc - te Spi - ri - tus, O ve - ni, ve - ni,
T
B

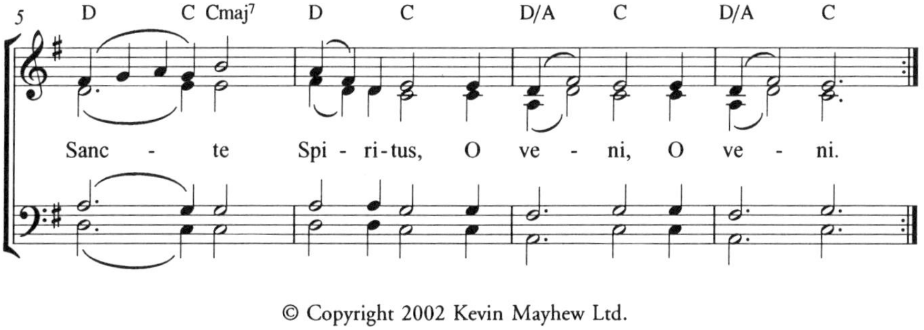
5
D C Cmaj7 D C D/A C D/A C
Sanc - te Spi - ri-tus, O ve - ni, O ve - ni.

MAGNIFICAT

My soul praises and magnifies the Lord

Text: Luke 1: 46

Music: Margaret Rizza

Andante (♩ = 100)
Am E Am/C E F
S A
T B
Mag - ni - fi - cat, mag - ni - fi - cat a - ni - ma
6
C Dm E A E
me - a Do - mi - num. Mag - ni - fi - cat,
11
F C F C Dm
mag - ni - fi - cat a - ni - ma me - a Do - mi -
Last time
rit. al fine
16
E Am Dm Esus4 E A
Fine
num. a - ni - ma me - a, Do - mi - num.

A lower setting

Andante (♩ = 100)
Gm D Gm/B♭ D E♭
S A
T B
Mag - ni - fi - cat, mag - ni - fi - cat a - ni - ma
6
B♭ Cm D G D
me - a Do - mi - num. Mag - ni - fi - cat,
11
E♭ B♭ E♭ B♭ Cm
mag - ni - fi - cat a - ni - ma me - a Do - mi -
16
Last time
rit. al fine
D Gm Cm Dsus4 D G
Fine
num. a - ni - ma me - a, Do - mi - num.

KYRIE, ELEISON

Lord, have mercy. Christ, have mercy. Lord, hear us
Christ, have mercy. Lord, have mercy. Christ, hear us

Text: Traditional
Music: Margaret Rizza

(𝅗𝅥 = 56)
Em F#m7(b5) Em Am/C D
S
A
Ky - ri - e, e - le - i - son. Chri - ste, e - le - i - son.
T
B
5
G Bm7 G Am7 Am6 Gmaj7 G6 Em/G Bsus4 B
Ky - ri - e, ex - au - di nos, Do - mi - ne.
9
Em Em7/D Cmaj7 D G/B C Am6 B
Ky - ri - e, e - le - i - son. Chri - ste, e - le - i - son.
13
Em Em7/D Am7 D Bm7 G
Ky - ri - e, e - le - i - son. Chri - ste, ex -

16
Am7 Am6 Gmaj7 G6 Em/G Bsus4 B
au - di nos, Do - mi - ne.
Last time
19
rall. al fine
Em F#m7(b5) Em
Ky - ri - e, Ky - ri - e, Do - mi - ne,
rall. al fine
22
F#m7(b5) Em F#m7/E E
Fine
Do - mi - ne, Do - mi - ne!

SANCTUS DOMINUS

Holy Lord God of hosts

Text: Traditional
Music: Margaret Rizza

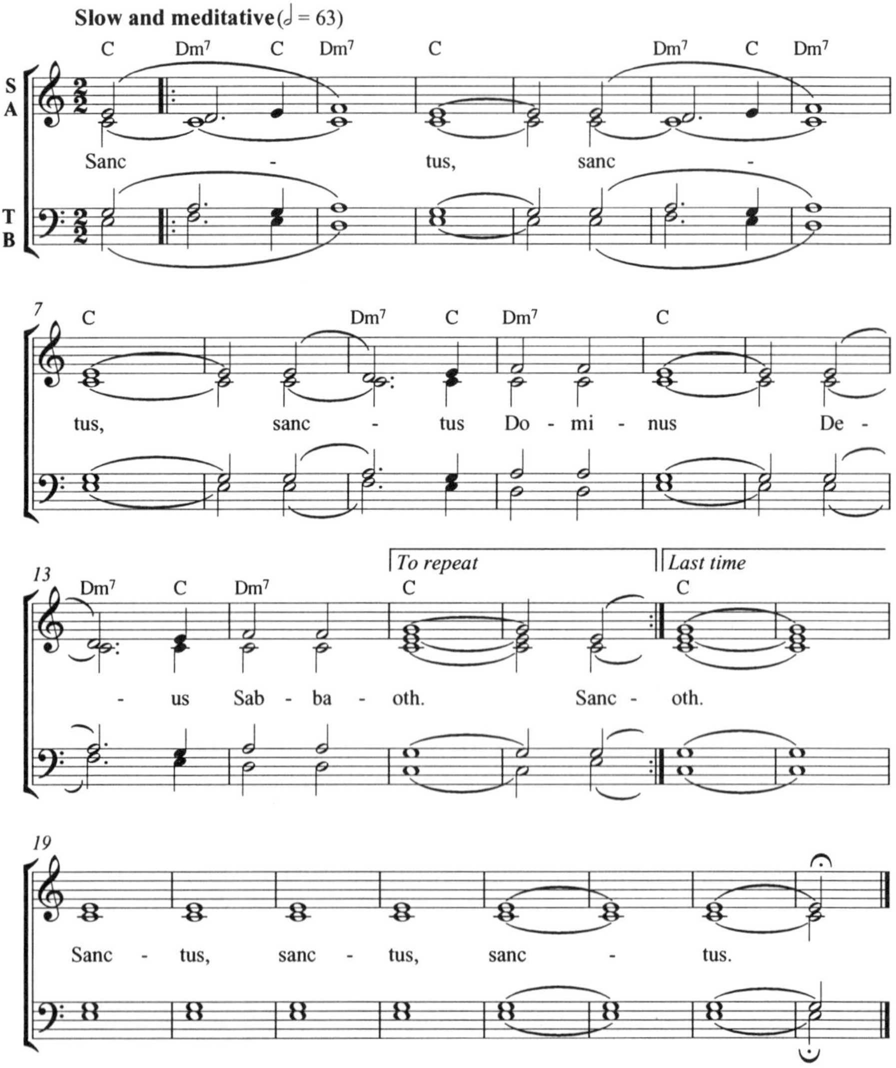

Slow and meditative (♩ = 63)
C Dm7 C Dm7 C Dm7 C Dm7
S A
T B
Sanc - tus, sanc -
7
C Dm7 C Dm7 C
tus, sanc - tus Do - mi - nus De -
13
To repeat
Last time
Dm7 C Dm7 C C
- us Sab - ba - oth. Sanc - oth.
19
Sanc - tus, sanc - tus, sanc - tus.

GETHSEMANE

My soul is ready to die with sorrow.
Sit down here while I go to pray. Stay here and keep watch.

Text: adapted from Matthew 26:36-38
Music: Margaret Rizza

Slow (♩ = 60)
Dm Em7 Am B♭maj7 Em7(♭5) Asus4 A Dm Gm9 Em7(♭5) Dm Asus4 A
S
A
Tris - tis est a - ni-ma me - a, us - que ad mor-tem, us - que ad mor-tem; se -
T
B
5
Dm Gm7 C F Gm9 Em7(♭5) Dm Asus4 A
de-te hic, don - nec o - rem, sus - ti - ne - te hic et vi - gi - la - te.
Last time
9
Dm Em7 Dm Em7(♭5) Dm Em7
rall. e dim. al fine
Tris - tis est a - ni - ma me - a, tris - tis est
rall. e dim. al fine
12
Dm Em7(♭5) Dm Em7 Dm
a - ni - ma me - a.

SILENT SURRENDERED

Text: v.1: Pamela Hayes; v.2: Margaret Rizza
Music: Margaret Rizza

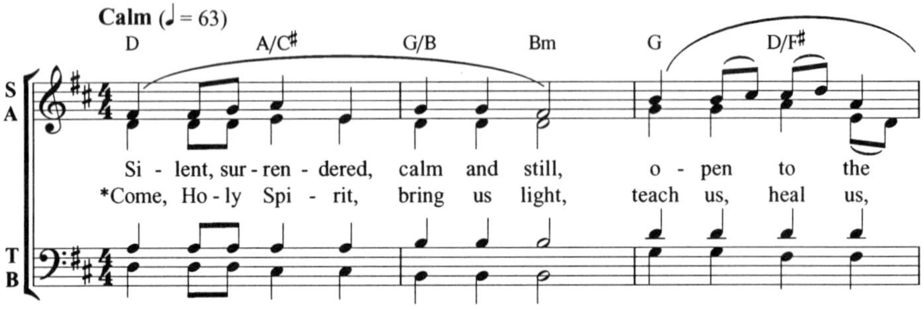
Calm (♩ = 63)
D A/C♯ G/B Bm G D/F♯
S A
Si - lent, sur - ren - dered, calm and still, o - pen to the
*Come, Ho - ly Spi - rit, bring us light, teach us, heal us,
T B

* *Additional verse for Pentecost*

4
Em7 A7 D A/C♯ Bm A7
word of God. Heart hum - bled to his will,
give us life. Come, Lord, O let our hearts

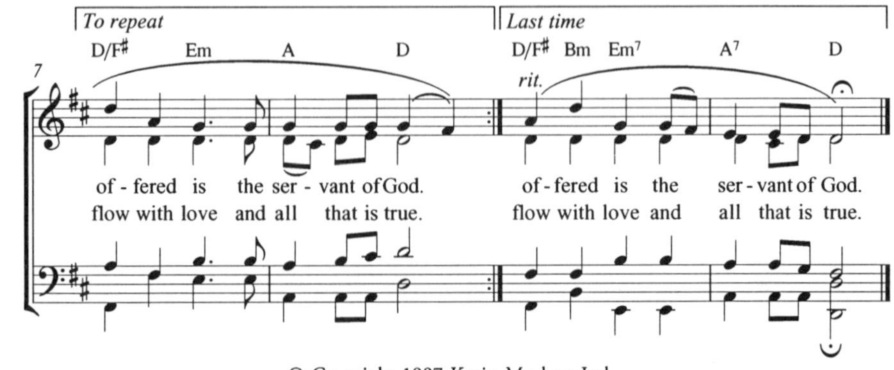
To repeat
Last time
7
D/F♯ Em A D D/F♯ Bm Em7 A7 D
rit.
of - fered is the ser - vant of God. of - fered is the ser - vant of God.
flow with love and all that is true. flow with love and all that is true.

A lower setting

Calm (♩ = 63)
C G/B F/A Am F C/E
S A
T B
Si - lent, sur - ren - dered, calm and still, o - pen to the
*Come, Ho - ly Spi - rit, bring us light, teach us, heal us,
4 Dm7 G7 C G/B Am G7
word of God. Heart hum - bled to his will,
give us life. Come, Lord, O let our hearts
To repeat
Last time
C/E Dm G C
C/E Am Dm7 G7 C
7
rit.
of - fered is the ser - vant of God.
flow with love and all that is true.
of - fered is the ser - vant of God.
flow with love and all that is true.

* *Additional verse for Pentecost*

PRAYER OF ST PATRICK

Jesus, Lord

Text: after St Patrick
Music: Margaret Rizza

Very calm, meditatively (♩ = 76)
S A
T B
Am7 Em7 Am7 Em7
Je - su Do - mi - ne, Je - su Do - mi - ne.
5
Je - su Do-mi-ne, Je - su Do - mi - ne.
Je - su Do - mi - ne, Je - su Do - mi - ne.
Final Chant
Last time
dim. e rall. al fine
9
Je - su Do - mi - ne, Je - su Do - mi - ne.
dim. e rall. al fine
Je - su Do - mi - ne, Je - su Do - mi - ne.
dim. e rall. al fine

BENEDICTUS

Blessed is he who comes in the name of the Lord

Text: Traditional
Music: Margaret Rizza

Largo (♩ = 69)
F Fmaj7 Dm Dm7 Gm C C7 F B♭maj7 Edim A Aaug
S
A
Be - ne - dic - tus qui ve - nit in no - mi - ne Do - mi - ni,
T
B

To repeat
5
Dm Dm7 B♭ C7 Am Dm Gm Csus4 C
be - ne - dic - tus qui ve - nit in no - mi - ne Do - mi - ni.

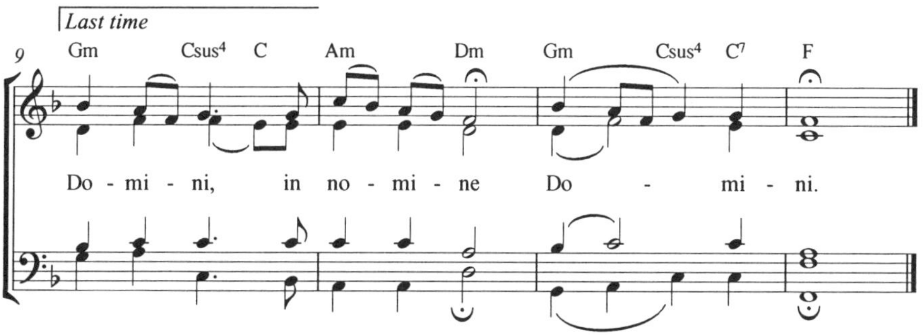
Last time
9
Gm Csus4 C Am Dm Gm Csus4 C7 F
Do - mi - ni, in no - mi - ne Do - mi - ni.

KEEP WATCH WITH ME

Text: Traditional
Music: Margaret Rizza

Harmony 1
Flowing (♩ = 66)
D Gm Am7(♭5) Gm Am7(♭5) Dm E♭maj7 Cm Cm7 D D7/C
S
A
Keep watch with me, pray with me and do not be a - fraid; keep
T
B
5
Gm Cm Am7 Am6 Gm Cm7 Am/C Cm7 Dsus4 D
watch with me, pray with me and do not be a - fraid; keep
Last time
9
Gm Am7(♭5) G Cm7 Dsus4 D G
watch with me, pray with me, do not be a - fraid.

Harmony 2

D Gm Am7(b5) Gm Dsus4 Dm E♭ Cm7 D D7
S
A
Keep watch with me, pray with me and do not be a - fraid; keep
T
B
5
Gm Cm Am7(b5) Gm Cm7 Am7(b5) Dsus4 D
watch with me, pray with me and do not be a - fraid; keep
Last time
9
Gm Am7(b5) Gm Cm7 Dsus4 D G
watch with me, pray with me, do not be a - fraid.

IN THE LORD IS MY JOY

Text and Music: Margaret Rizza

Andante (♩ = c.76)
S
A
T
B
Cm Fm7 B♭ E♭maj7 A♭ Fm
In the Lord is my joy and sal - va - tion, he gives light to
4
Gsus4 G Cm Fm7 B♭ E♭maj7
all his cre - a - tion. In the Lord is my joy and sal - va - tion,
7
A♭ Fm Gsus4 G Cm
he gives peace and true con - so - la - tion.
9
Final Chant
Cm Fm7 B♭ E♭maj7 A♭ Gsus4 G
In the Lord is my sal - va - tion.
13
Cm Fm7 B♭ E♭maj7 A♭ Fm Gsus4 G C
dim. e rall. al fine
In the Lord is my sal - va - tion.

A lower setting

Andante (♩ = c.76)
S
A
T
B
Bm Em7 A Dmaj7 G Em
In the Lord is my joy and sal - va - tion, he gives light to
F#sus4 F# Bm Em7 A Dmaj7
all his cre - a - tion. In the Lord is my joy and sal - va - tion,
G Em F#sus4 F# Bm
he gives peace and true con - so - la - tion.
Final Chant
Bm Em7 A Dmaj7 G F#sus4 F#
In the Lord is my sal - va - tion.
Bm Em7 A Dm7 G Em F#sus4 F# B
dim. e rall. al fine
In the Lord is my sal - va - tion.

INPOURED SPIRIT

Text: Pamela Hayes
Music: Margaret Rizza

Andante (♩ = 80)
TRIO: add a part on each repetition
Capo 1
E♭ D
Fm7 Em7
E♭ D
A♭ G
1: Altos
In - poured Spi - rit, deep and still,
2: Sopranos
In - poured Spi - rit deep and still,
3: Men
In - poured Spi - rit deep and still,
E♭ D
Cm Bm
Fm7 Em7
B♭sus4 Asus4
B♭ A
love e - ter - nal the world to fill.
love e - ter - nal the world to fill.
love e - ter - nal the world to fill.
Last time
In - poured Spi - rit, deep and still,
love e - ter - nal the world to fill.

ADORAMUS TE, DOMINE DEUS

We adore you, O Lord God

Text: Traditional
Music: Margaret Rizza

Slow and calm (𝅗𝅥 = c.52)
F Gm7/F F7 Gm7/F F Gm7/F F7 Gm7/F
S A
A - do - ra - mus te, Do - mi - ne De - us.
T B
5
F Gm7/F F7 Gm7/F F Gm7/F F7 Gm11/F
A - do - ra - mus te, Do - mi - ne De - us.
Last time
F Gm11/F F Gm11/F F Gm7 F
9
A - do - ra - mus te, a - do - ra - mus te, a - do - ra - mus te.
Hum

A BLESSING

Text: Gaelic Blessing, adapted by Margaret Rizza
Music: Margaret Rizza

(♩ = c.63)
G C G D Em Am7
S A
May the Lord bless you, may the Lord pro - tect you and
T B
4
Dsus4 D D7 Bm7 G C D7 Bm
guide you, may his strength up - hold you, his light shine up -
7
Em Em7 C G C D7sus4 D7
on you, his peace sur - round you, his love en - fold you.
Last time
dim e rall. al fine
10
G C G C G C G
May the Lord bless you, the Lord bless you, the Lord bless you.

A lower setting

(♩ = c.63)
S
A
T
B
F Bb F C Dm Gm7
May the Lord bless you, may the Lord pro-tect you and
4
Csus4 C C7 Am7 F Bb C7 Am
guide you, may his strength up-hold you, his light shine up-
7
Dm Dm7 Bb F Bb Csus4 C7
on you, his peace sur-round you, his love en-fold you.
Last time
10
F Bb F Bb F Bb F
dim. e rall. al fine
May the Lord bless you, the Lord bless you, the Lord bless you.

O LORD, MY HEART IS NOT PROUD

Text: Psalm 131
Music: Margaret Rizza

Calm (♩ = 66)
A D A/C♯ Bm Em7 Asus4 A
S A
O Lord, my heart is not proud, nor haugh - ty my eyes.
T B
5
D A/C♯ G/B F♯/A♯ Bm Em7 Asus4 A
I have not gone af - ter things too great, nor mar - vels be - yond me.
9
G A7/G D/F♯ Bm Em Em/D A/C♯ A
Tru-ly I have set my soul in si - lence and peace; at

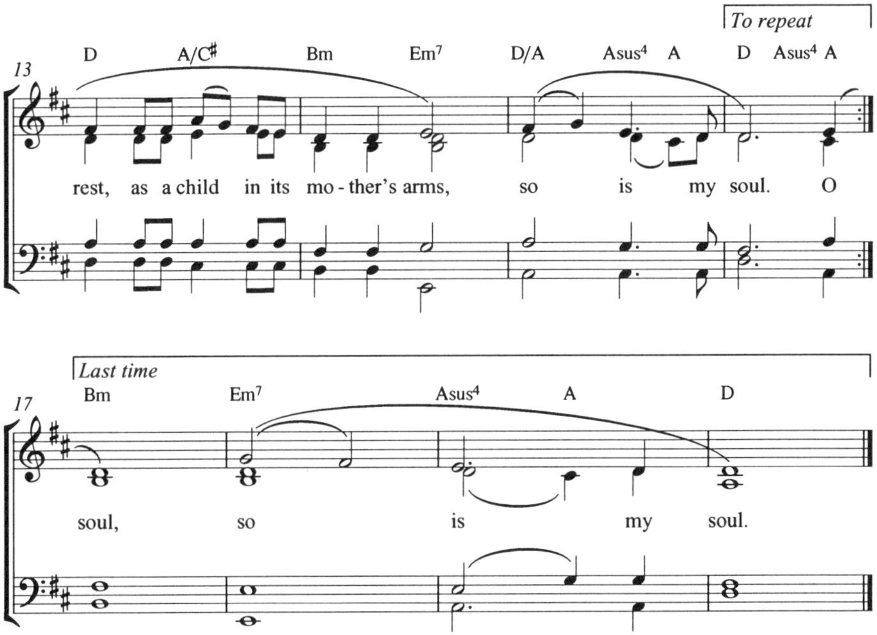
13
To repeat
D A/C♯ Bm Em7 D/A Asus4 A D Asus4 A
rest, as a child in its mo - ther's arms, so is my soul. O
Last time
17
Bm Em7 Asus4 A D
soul, so is my soul.

A lower setting

Calm (♩ = 66)
G C G/B Am Dm7 Gsus4 G
S
A
O Lord, my heart is not proud, nor haugh - ty my eyes.
T
B
5
C G/B F/A E/G♯ Am Dm7 Gsus4 G
I have not gone af - ter things too great, nor mar - vels be - yond me.
9
F G7/F C/E Am Dm Dm/C G/B G
(,)
Tru-ly I have set my soul in si - lence and peace; at
(,)

To repeat
C G/B Am Dm7 C/G Gsus4 G C G
13
rest, as a child in its mo - ther's arms, so is my soul. O

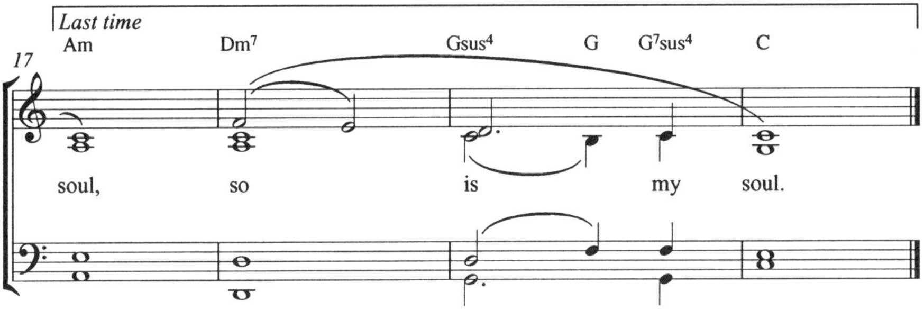
Last time
Am Dm7 Gsus4 G G7sus4 C
17
soul, so is my soul.

VENI, LUMEN CORDIUM

Come, light of our hearts. Come, Holy Spirit, come

Text: Stephen Langton (d.1228)
Music: Margaret Rizza

(♪ = c.120)
S A T B
Em Am Dsus4 Gmaj7 C Em/G Am B
Ve - ni, lu - men cor - di - um. Ve - ni, San - cte Spi - ri - tus.
Em Am Dsus4 Gmaj7 C Em/G Am B
Ve - ni, lu - men cor - di - um. Ve - ni, San - cte Spi - ri - tus.
Final chant
Em Am Dsus4 Gmaj7 C Em/G Am B
Ve - ni, lu - men cor - di - um.
Em Am Dsus4 Gmaj7 C Am Bsus4 B E
rall. al fine
Ve - ni, San - cte Spi - ri - tus. A - men.
rall. al fine

EXAUDI NOS, DOMINE

Hear us, O Lord; give us your peace

Text and Music: Margaret Rizza

THE LORD IS MY LIGHT

Text: From Psalm 27
Music: Margaret Rizza

Larghetto (♩ = c.76-80)
S
A
T
B
G Am Am7/G Dm7/F G7/F Em7 C/E
The Lord is my light, my hope, my sal-va - tion; in him I trust, in
5
G7sus4 G Am Am7/G Dm7/F G7/F
him I trust. There is one thing I ask of the Lord: for this I long, to
8
Em7 C/E G7sus4 G Am Am7/G
live in his house all the days of my life; to sa - vour the sweet-ness, the
11
Dm7/F G7/F Em7 C/E G7sus4 G
sweet-ness of the Lord; to be - hold his tem - ple; for this I long. The

Am Am7/G Dm7/F G7/F Em7 C/E
14
Lord is my light, my hope, my sal - va - tion; in him I trust, in
To repeat
Last time
rall. e dim. al fine
G7sus4 G G Am Am7/G Fmaj7 G7/F
17
him I trust. The him I trust. The Lord is my light, in
rall. e dim. al fine
Em7 C/E Dm9 Dm7 C Dm7/C
21
him I trust. The Lord is my light, in
C Dm7/C C Dm/C C G7sus4 C
26
Fine
him I trust, in him I trust.

A lower setting

Larghetto (♩ = c.76-80)
F Gm Gm7/F Cm7/E♭ F7/E♭ Dm7 B♭
S A
T B
The Lord is my light, my hope, my sal-va - tion; in him I trust, in
F7sus4 F Gm Gm7/F Cm7/E♭ F7/E♭
5
him I trust. There is one thing I ask of the Lord: for this I long, to
Dm7 B♭/D F7sus4 F Gm Gm7/F
8
live in his house all the days of my life; to sa - vour the sweet-ness, the
Cm7/E♭ F7/E♭ Dm7 B♭ F7sus4 F
11
sweet-ness of the Lord; to be - hold his tem - ple; for this I long. The

14
Gm Gm7/F Gm7/E♭ F7/E♭ Dm7 B♭/D
Lord is my light, my hope, my sal - va - tion; in him I trust, in
To repeat
Last time
rall. e dim. al fine
17
F7sus4 F F7sus4 F Gm Gm7 E♭maj7 F7
him I trust. The him I trust. The Lord is my light, in
rall. e dim. al fine
21
Dm7 B♭/D Cm9 Cm7 B♭ Cm7/B♭
him I trust. The Lord is my light, in
26
B♭ Cm7/B♭ B♭ Cm/B♭ B♭ F7sus4 B♭
Fine
him I trust, in him I trust.

CALM ME, LORD

Text: David Adam
Music: Margaret Rizza

Tranquil (♩ = 108)
D A/C♯ Bm Bm11 Bm
S
A
Calm me, Lord, as you calmed the storm;
T
B
5
G D Em7 Asus4 A D
still me, Lord, keep me from harm. Let all the
10
A/C♯ Bm G/B D/A
tu - mult with - in me cease; en - fold me,
To repeat
Last time
14
Bm Em7 Asus4 A Bm Em7 Asus4 A D
Lord, in your peace. Lord, en - fold me in your peace.

A lower setting

Tranquil (♩ = 108)
S
A
T
B
C G/B Am Am11 Am
Calm me, Lord, as you calmed the storm;
5
F C/E Dm7 Gsus4 G C
still me, Lord, keep me from harm. Let all the
10
G/B Am F/A C/G
tu - mult with - in me cease; en - fold me,
To repeat
Last time
14
Am Dm7 Gsus4 G Am Dm7 Gsus4 G C
Lord, in your peace. Lord, en - fold me in your peace.

SANCTUM NOMEN

My soul magnifies the holy name of the Lord

Text: Traditional

Music: Margaret Rizza

JESU CHRISTE

Music: Margaret Rizza

CHRISTUS NATUS EST

Alleluia, Glory to God on high.
Christ is born of the Virgin Mary

Text: Traditional
Music: Margaret Rizza

First Chant
(♩ = c.72)
N.C.
S
A
T
B
Chris - tus na - tus est, Chris - tus na - tus est,
Am7 Bm C Cmaj7 Am6 Bm7 Em Bsus4 Bm7 Em7
ex Ma - ri - a Vir - gi - ne, glo-ri - a in ex-cel - sis De - o.
N.C.
Al - le - lu - ia, glo-ri - a, al - le - lu - ia, glo-ri - a.

Second Chant

For Samuel, our first grandchild

A CELTIC BLESSING

Text: Traditional
Music: Margaret Rizza

(♩ = 69)
D Bm/D Em7 A7sus4 A
S
The guard-ing of the God of Life be on you, the
A
The guard - ing of God, the
T
B
3
Bm Bm7 Em Am Am7 D/F# Bm
guard - ing of lov-ing Christ be on you, the guard-ing of the Ho-ly Spi-rit
guard - ing of Christ, the guard - ing of the
6
Em7 A7 Dmaj7 Bm Em7 A
Last time
be on you, to aid and up-hold you each day and night of your life;
Spi - rit be up - on you; the

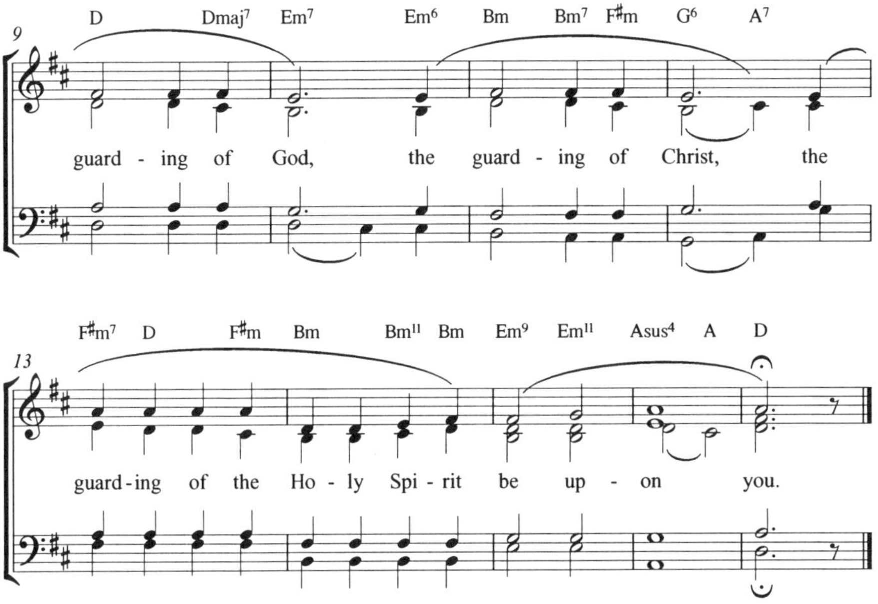
D Dmaj7 Em7 Em6 Bm Bm7 F♯m G6 A7
9
guard - ing of God, the guard - ing of Christ, the
F♯m7 D F♯m Bm Bm11 Bm Em9 Em11 Asus4 A D
13
guard - ing of the Ho - ly Spi - rit be up - on you.

In memory of 11th September 2001

O DOMINE, O CHRISTE

O Lord, O Christ, give us peace

Text: Traditional
Music: Margaret Rizza

(♩ = 69)
O Do - mi - ne, O Chris - te,
Em7 Am D♯dim Em7 Am7 D
S
A
O Do - mi - ne, O Chris - te,
T
B
3
G Am7 Am6 Em/G B7sus4 B7 Em7 Am7
O Do-mi - ne,
Do - na no - bis pa - cem. O Do-mi - ne,
O Chris - te,
6
D7 Gmaj7 C Cmaj7/F♯ B7sus4 B7
O Chris - te, do - na no - bis pa - cem.

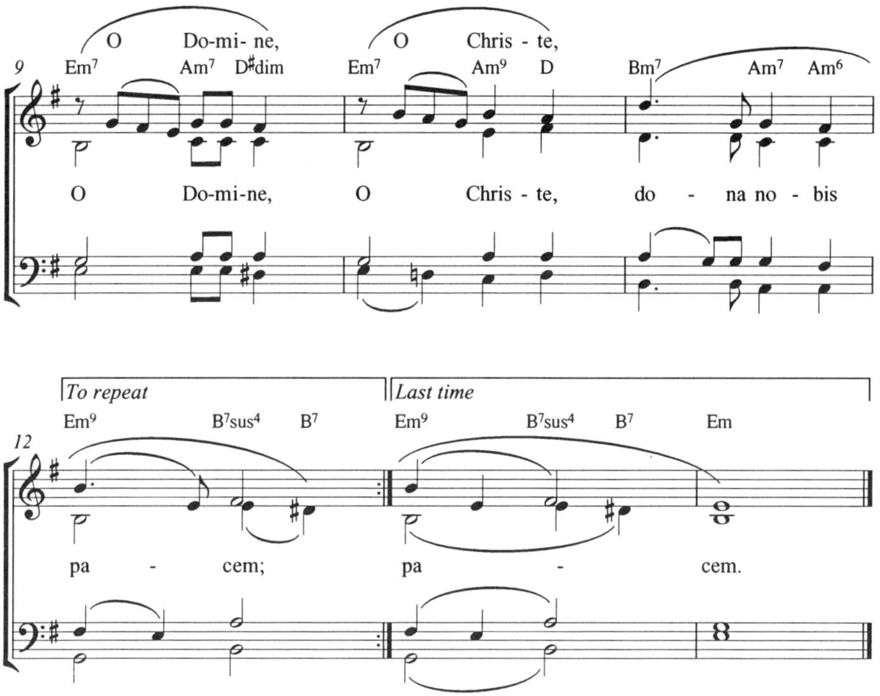
O Do-mi- ne, O Chris - te,
9
Em7 Am7 D#dim Em7 Am9 D Bm7 Am7 Am6
O Do-mi-ne, O Chris - te, do - na no - bis
To repeat
Last time
Em9 B7sus4 B7 Em9 B7sus4 B7 Em
12
pa - cem; pa - cem.

O GIVE THANKS TO THE LORD

Text: from Psalm 118
Music: Margaret Rizza

O LORD LISTEN TO MY PRAYER

Text: from Psalm 101(102)
Music: Margaret Rizza

B7 Em F#m7(b5) Em7 Am7 D
(♩ = 80)
S
A
O Lord lis - ten to my prayer, my prayer as I call to
T
B
Gmaj7 C F#m7(b5) B7sus4 B7 Bm7
you; O Lord lis - ten to my prayer, my
To repeat
Last time
Em/G Am7 B Em Em
prayer as I call to you. O you.

Also available from Kevin Mayhew

All the chants contained in this book (with the exception of *Christus natus est, Gethsemane, Jesu Christe* and *Prayer of St Patrick)* can be found on these CDs.

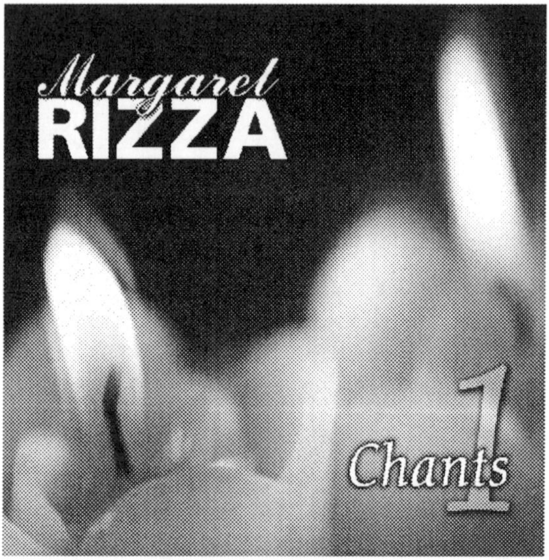

CD - 1490102

CD - 1490115
CASS - 1480092